ANTHEMS
FOR
MEN'S VOICES

edited by

Peter le Huray

Nicholas Temperley

Peter Tranchell

David Willcocks

VOLUME I

Altos, Tenors and Basses

OXFORD UNIVERSITY PRESS

MUSIC DEPARTMENT 44 CONDUIT STREET LONDON W.1

CONTENTS—*VOLUME I*

Chorus parts are shown by capital letters, solo parts in lower case.
O indicates organ accompaniment. Optional parts are shown in brackets.
* Anthems so marked can be sung, with suitable transposition, by a men's choir
without altos. In the anthem marked † only the first part may be sung in that way.

KEY

Ad—Advent As—Ascension C—Christmas D—Dedication Ea—Easter Ep—Epiphany
F—Funeral G—General L—Lent P—Passion Q—Quinquagesima S—Saints' Days
Sep—Septuagesima Th—Thanksgiving Tr—Trinity W—Whitsun

PREFACE

THE AIM of this book is to present a selection of anthems for men's voices, for use in cathedrals, chapels, churches and schools.

Volume 1 is for altos, tenors and basses; Volume 2 for tenors and basses. Some of the anthems (marked * in the Contents) for the one kind of choir would, if transposed, be suitable for the other.

The selection is designed to enlarge the male voice repertoire as much as possible. It is therefore drawn wholly from these three categories:

1. Anthems hitherto existing only in manuscript.
2. Anthems at some time in print, but not now available.
3. Anthems now in print, but only available in collected editions.

The music chosen is all from the period c. 1450 to c. 1800. Several hundred pieces, of all periods, were considered for inclusion. The 19th and 20th centuries are not represented because of the relative dearth of suitable anthems in the three categories mentioned. The editors have tried as far as possible to provide music for the main seasons and feasts of the Church year, and to achieve variety of musical character. An anthem of musical interest but with an unsuitable text will have been excluded rather than provided with another text. Some anthems are underlaid with translations of their original German or Italian texts. A literal translation of Latin texts (not intended for use in performance) is provided, except where one may easily be found by reference to the appropriate verses in the Bible or Psalter.

Where an anthem is an extract from a longer work, the work is named in the footnote which states the textual sources consulted. In a few cases an anthem, otherwise too long for the purposes of this book, has been shortened by the omission of a verse or other section.

Some anthems have been transposed. The original pitch may be seen (together with the original clefs and signatures) before the first bar of each anthem.

All editorial emendations and additions including realisations of figured basses are shown in small type; emendations are also mentioned in footnotes. Editorial ornaments and other suggestions for performance are shown in square brackets. The verbal text appears in square brackets if it is absent in the original, in italics if the original text has been altered or if it varies between sources. Where the underlay is editorial it is indicated by crossed slurs.

The music is printed in modern notation and the verbal texts normally in roman type. Variants between sources are shown in an appendix. Editorial slurs and ties have a cross stroke : ⌒⊦⌒ . Accidentals in round brackets are cautionary reminders by the editors. Accidentals in square brackets indicate a variance between the sources.

The following conventions are used in footnotes and in the lists of variants. Reference is by Anthem no. (if necessary) in bold figures, bar number, part (A1 for first alto, etc.; rh for right hand, etc.), and number of symbol (including rests) in the bar (a note tied to the preceding bar being reckoned as 0); thus, **12** 26. T2. 2 would refer to Anthem 12, bar 26, second tenor part, second note (or rest). What follows the reference is usually a description of some aspect of the original, beginning at the point indicated and continuing until the original ceases to differ from the version printed. Note values are shown by lower case italics (*s* for semibreve, *m.* for dotted minim, etc.) and pitches by capital letters, using the time and pitch scales of the present version, not those of the original. The sign O means that the original note had no accidental. Sources, if more than one, are listed and numbered on the first page of each anthem, and are then referred to by these numbers in round brackets.

ACKNOWLEDGEMENTS

This book could not have been printed without the interest and generosity of the Masters and Fellows of two Colleges: Clare College, and Gonville and Caius College, Cambridge, England. The editors are particularly grateful to the Master of Clare College, Sir Eric Ashby, for his encouragement. They also record their thanks to Mr George Guest, Mr Raymond Leppard and Dr John Cockshoot for suggesting anthems for inclusion, and to Mr J. Merill Knapp whose book 'Selected List of Music for Men's Voices' (Princeton, 1952) directed them to some of the anthems here printed.

Their gratitude is also due to the Rev. Professor Ratcliff for assistance in the identification of Latin texts, and to Mr Charles Cudworth for his help in locating sources; to Dr Rosamund Harding for her advice as regards dating and for provision of photocopies of anthems by Locke; and to Miss Margaret Balmforth, Mr Brian Runnett and Mr John Langdon for their kind assistance in the work of transcription.

Cambridge, 1965

INDEX FOR SEASONS AND OCCASIONS

ANTHEMS FOR MEN'S VOICES
Volume One

1. HEAR THE VOICE AND PRAYER

I Kings 8, vv. 28-30

THOMAS TALLIS
(*c.* 1505-1585)

Sources: (1) Oxford, Bodleian Library, MSS. Mus. Sch. e. 420-2 (*c.* 1549)
(2) John Day, *Certaine Notes* (London, *c.* 1565)
(3) London, British Museum, Add. MSS. 30480-4 (*c.* 1580)
(4) New York Public Library, MSS. Drexel 4180-5 (*c.* 1625)

© Oxford University Press 1965

Printed in Great Britain

OXFORD UNIVERSITY PRESS, MUSIC DEPARTMENT, 44 CONDUIT STREET, LONDON, W.1

14

that thine eyes may o - pen to - ward this house night and day, *ev - en to - ward this*

house *night and day,* *to - ward this* house night and day, ev - en to - ward this

to - ward this house night and day, night and day, *ev - en to - ward this*

eyes may o - pen to - ward this house night and day, *ev - en to - ward this*

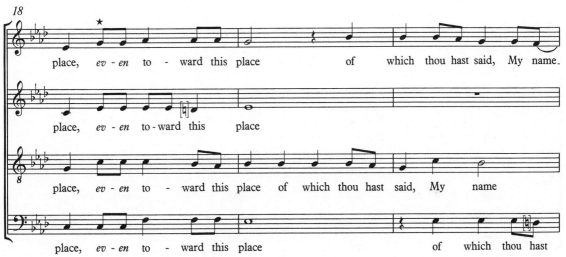

18

place, *ev - en to - ward this place* of which thou hast said, My name

place, *ev - en to - ward this place*

place, *ev - en to - ward this place* of which thou hast said, My name

place, *ev - en to - ward this place* of which thou hast

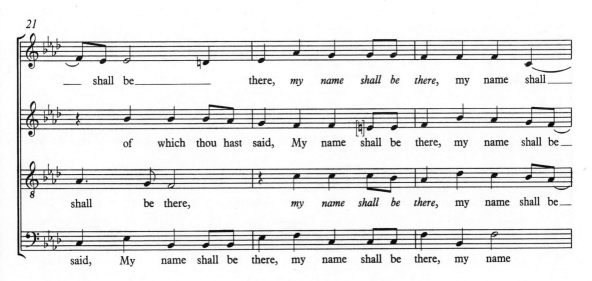

21

shall be there, *my name shall be there,* my name shall

of which thou hast said, My name shall be there, my name shall be

shall be there, *my name shall be there,* my name shall be

said, My name shall be there, my name shall be there, my name

★ever

4

2. SUBMIT YOURSELVES

Ephesians 5, vv. 21, 19, 20

JOHN SHEPHERD
(*c.* 1520–*c.* 1563)

Sources: (1) Oxford, Bodleian Library, MSS. Mus. Sch. e. 420-2 (*c.* 1549)
(2) John Day, *Certaine Notes* (London, *c.* 1565)
(3) New York Public Library, MSS. Drexel 4180-5 (*c.* 1625)

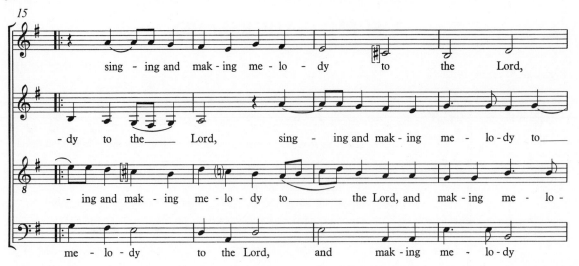

3. IERUSALEM, CONVERTERE AD DOMINUM

From the Second Nocturn
for Maundy Thursday

G. P. da PALESTRINA
(1525-1594)

Source: G.P. da Palestrina, *Lamentationes* (Rome, 1588)
Meaning of text: *Jerusalem, turn thou unto the Lord thy God.*

4. HE THAT HATH MY COMMANDMENTS

John 14, v. 21

[WILLIAM] MUNDY
(*c.* 1529–*c.* 1591)

Sources: (1) New York, Drexel MSS. 4180-3 (*c.* 1625)
(2) Durham Cathedral, MSS. A3, C11, C17 (*c.* 1630)
(3) London, British Museum, Add. MS. 30478, ff. 77-78 (*c.* 1660)
Minor rhythmic discrepancies between organ and voices have been retained: the organ part occurs in source (2) only. The layout for r.h. and l.h. is as in the original.
Bars 1-14 of this anthem may be used separately as an introit.

★The following alterations will avoid the low second alto part in bars 9, 10 and 14:
  A. 2: bar 9, sing B crotchet on *he*, then take T. part until bar 14.
  T: bars 9–14, take A. 2 part.

Anthems for men's voices (Vol. I)

★As there is no simple way of avoiding the low notes in bars 19-20, it is suggested that the second altos be supported by one or two tenors and basses in these bars.

32. Al. 1-2: *c.q*

There are no repeat marks in source (1)

5. LET US NOW LAUD

Words anon.

WILLIAM MUNDY
(c. 1529–c. 1591)

Sources: (1) New York Public Library, MSS. Drexel 4180-3 (c. 1625)
(2) London, British Museum, Add. MS. 29289 (c. 1630)
(3) Durham Cathedral, MSS. A3, C11, C17 (c. 1635)
(4) London, British Museum, Add. MS. 30478 (c. 1660)

Minor rhythmic discrepancies between organ and voices have been retained. The layout for r.h. and l.h. is as in the original. The organ part occurs in source (3) only.

18

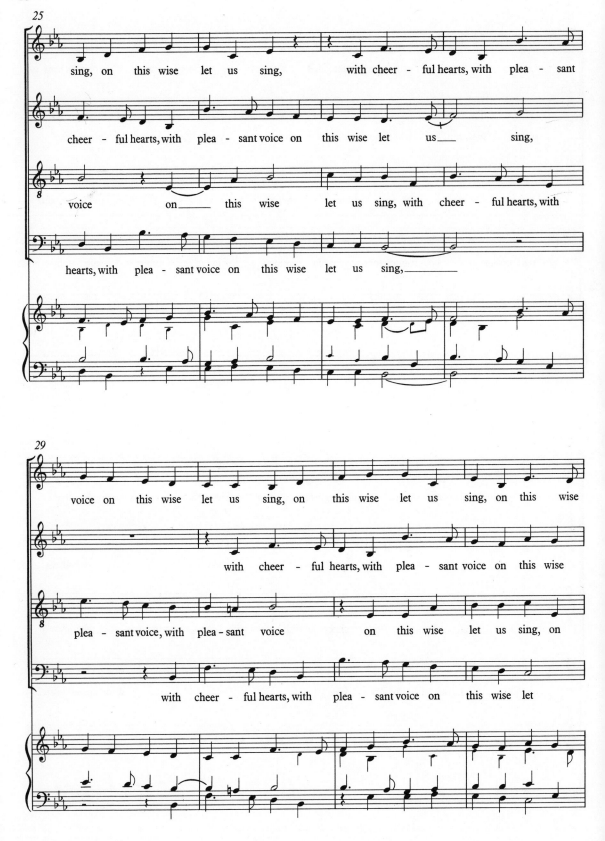

6. BE UNTO ME, O LORD, A TOWER

WILLIAM BYRD
(1543-1623)

Words anon.

Source: Sir William Leighton, *The Teares or Lamentacions of a Sorrowfull Soule* (London, 1614).

The underlay is often ambiguous in the original.

7. DEO GRATIAS

Early Christian Grace

WILLIAM BYRD
(1543-1623)

Source: Gradualia, Book I (1605), Part 1, no. 20
Meaning of text: *Thanks be to God*

8. GLORIA TIBI, DOMINE

Verse 5 of the hymn *Quem terra pontus*,
attrib. Venantius Fortunatus (6th cent.)

WILLIAM BYRD
(1543-1623)

Source: Gradualia, Book I (1605), Part 3, no. 1 (*Quem terra pontus*), v. 5 and Amen.
Meaning of text: *Glory be to thee, O Lord, | Who wast born of a Virgin, | And to the Father and to the Holy Spirit | For ever and ever.*

9. VENI, SANCTE SPIRITUS, REPLE

Alleluia of the Mass on Whitsunday (Roman Use)
or on Whit Tuesday (Sarum Use)

WILLIAM BYRD
(1543-1623)

Source: Gradualia, Book II (1607), no. 33.

Meaning of text: *Come, Holy Spirit, fill the hearts of thy faithful; and kindle in them the fire of thy love. Alleluia.*

10. ECCE ADVENIT

Antiphon to the Introit
of the Mass on Epiphany

WILLIAM BYRD
(1543-1623)

Source: Gradualia, Book II (1607), no. 10, first section.

Meaning of text: *Behold, the Lord and Master hath come, with kingdom, power and dominion in his hand.*

11. VIRI GALILAEI

Acts I, v. 11. Antiphon to the Introit
of the Mass on Ascension Day

WILLIAM BYRD
(1543-1623)

Source: Gradualia, Book II (1607), no. 25, first section.

Meaning of text: *Men of Galilee, why look ye up to heaven in astonishment? Alleluia. In like manner as ye have seen him ascending into heaven, so shall he come again. Alleluia.*

12. VOCEM MEAM AUDISTI

From the Second Nocturn for Maundy Thursday
(Lamentations 3, vv. 56, 58)

ALPHONSO FERRABOSCO I
(1543-1588)

Source: London, British Museum, Egerton 3665 (early 17th c.), ff. 75v, 76.

13. ANTE LUCIFERUM GENITUS

Antiphon to the first Psalm of Lauds
on Epiphany, with an added *Alleluia*

JACOB HANDL, called GALLUS
(1550-1591)

Source: J. Handl, *Opus Musicum*, Tomus I (Prague, 1586), no. 56.

Meaning of text: *Begotten before the morning star, and Lord before all time, our Saviour hath this day appeared in the world. Alleluia.*

D with large natural represents B without accidental in the original; D without accidental (or with large flat contradicting natural) represents B with flat in the original; D with small flat represents B without accidental in the original which the editors recommend flattening.

14. HONESTUM FECIT

In communi de Martyribus

Wisdom 10, vv. 12, 14
Part of the Lesson in the Mass
Pro Martyre non Pontifice

JACOB HANDL, called GALLUS
(1550-1591)

Source: J. Handl, *Opus Musicum*, Tomus 4 (Prague, 1590), no. 119

Meaning of text: *The Lord hath made him to be honoured, and hath protected him from his enemies, and hath guarded him from tempters, and hath given him eternal renown.*

15. LET MY COMPLAINT

Psalm 119, vv. 169-176, and Gloria

THOMAS MORLEY
(1557-1603)

Sources: (1) London, Royal College of Music, MSS. 1045-51 (c. 1625)
(2) Tenbury, St. Michael's College, MS. 791 (c. 1630)

The clefs and key-signatures of the full sections are: A, 'C'4, ♭; T, 'C'3, 2♭; B1 'C'2, ♭; B2, 'F'2, ♭; Org. 'C'4 & 'F'3.

The solo voice is silent in the choruses until bar 72. The anthem may be transposed up a tone and sung by alto solo and AATB chorus.

27—28: 'Commandments' is treated as a four-syllable word in the original.

28. T. 1-2: *cc*

Anthems for men's voices (Vol. I)

39.r.h.4—40.r.h.3: B♭mAc.Gq / 39.l.h.4—40.l.h.3: GcDmCc

16. BLESSED IS HE WHOSE UNRIGHTEOUSNESS IS FORGIVEN

Psalm 32, vv. 1, 2

THOMAS TOMKINS
(1572-1656)

Source: *Musica Deo Sacra* (London, 1668)

18. T. 2-3: CC   23. T. 4: A

54

17. HEAR MY PRAYER, O LORD

Psalm 102, vv. 1, 2

THOMAS TOMKINS
(1572-1656)

Source: *Musica Deo Sacra* (London, 1668)

18. OUT OF THE DEEP

Psalm 130, vv. 1, 2

THOMAS TOMKINS
(1572-1656)

Source: *Musica Deo Sacra* (London, 1668)

34. T. 5-6: CB

19. REMEMBER ME, O LORD

Psalm 106, v. 4

THOMAS TOMKINS
(1572-1656)

Source: *Musica Deo Sacra* (London, 1668)

Note: The organ part differs considerably in places from the voice parts. The variants have not been reconciled in order that a clearer picture of the alternatives may emerge.

62

15. A1. 5—19. A1. 2: Db*q* Db*q* Ab*c* Bb*c* C*c*, *q*—rest, Bb*sq* C*sq* Db*c*. C*q* Bb*c*. Ab*q* Eb*m*, *s*—rest (underlay uncertain)

15. A2. 2—16. A2. 2: Db*s* only / 17. A2. 2:♮

29. B. 3: missing   33. A2. 1-2: C*q*D*q*

20. O LORD, I LIFT MY HEART TO THEE

Words anon.

ORLANDO GIBBONS
(1583-1625)

Source: William Leighton, *The Teares or Lamentacions of a Sorrowfull Soule* (London, 1614)

21. IN THE BEGINNING, O LORD

Psalm 102, vv. 25-27
(Source of translation unknown)

MATTHEW LOCKE
(*c.* 1622-1677)

Source: British Museum, Add. MS. 31437, ff. 13v, 14 (Autograph)

Dr. Rosamond Harding believes this anthem to have been composed before 1660.

The repeat is shown in the source by the sign .ꞔ. over the beginning of bar 27.

20. B. 2. This note, having no word set to it in the original, may not have been intended to be sung; the composer may have copied it in error from the continuo stave below.

22. LET GOD ARISE

Psalm 68, vv. 1, 3
(Source of translation unknown)

MATTHEW LOCKE
(c. 1622-1677)

Source: British Museum, Add. MS. 31437, ff. 4v, 5 (Autograph)

Dr. Rosamond Harding believes this anthem to have been composed before 1660.

Bar 18 represents two bars of the original; bar 23, three. The time-signature in these bars is 3 and each contains three minims.

23. O LORD, HEAR MY PRAYER

Psalm 102, vv. 1, 2
(Source of translation unknown)

MATTHEW LOCKE
(*c.* 1622-1677)

Source: British Museum, Add. MS. 31437, ff. 12v-13 (Autograph)

Dr. Rosamond Harding believes this anthem to have been composed before 1660.

The first part (bars 1-13) is highly suitable as an introit, or to conclude prayers.

33, all parts: black long in orig.

24. IN GOD'S WORD WILL I REJOICE

Psalm 56, vv. 10, 11

HENRY PURCELL
(1659-1695)

Source: London, British Museum, Add. MS. 30931 (*c.* 1687). Part of "Be merciful unto me."

25. LORD, NOT TO US

Psalm 115, v. 1
(John Patrick, *A Century of Select Psalms*, 1684)

HENRY PURCELL
(1659-1695)

Source: London, British Museum, Add. MS. 30930 (*c.* 1680)

26. O REMEMBER NOT

HENRY PURCELL
(1659-1695)

Psalm 79, v. 8

Source: Cambridge, Fitzwilliam Museum, MS. 88 (*c.* 1680-2). Part of "Lord, how long wilt thou be angry?"

27. LABORAVI IN GEMITU MEO

Psalm 6, v. 6

ANTONIO CALDARA
(1670–1736)

Source: A. Caldara, *Motetti a due e tre voci . . . Opera Quarta* (Bologna, 1715)

When two figures appear side by side under one bass note, their position does not indicate when the chord should be changed.

40.org.2: The figure here looks more like 6♭ in the original, but 5♭ was probably meant.

OXFORD UNIVERSITY PRESS

VARIANTS—*VOLUME I*

Large numbers refer to anthems. Numbers in brackets refer to the sources listed at the foot of the first page of each anthem. Other abbreviations are as described in the Preface.

1 k-s open in (3) and (4), and in (2) apart from T / 6.A1.4–5: $mD\natural$ only (2,3,4) / 7.A1.2–8.A1.3: rests only (4) / 9.A1.1: $E\natural$ tied from 8 (4) / 9.A1.1–2: $mE\flat$(2) / 10.A2.3–11.A2.1: *cm* (2) / 11.A1.0–1: $qFqGcE\natural$ (2) / 12 &c: *may^{q}be^q* (2) / 14.T.1–3: $qE\flat qD\flat cC$ (2) / 14 &c: *toward this place* (4) / 14 &c: *toward* and *towards* (2) / 18.A2. 4–6: $cE\flat qDqD$ (3,4) / 18.T.5: A$\flat$ (2) / 21.T.1–2: *cc* (4) / 21.A1.2–3: $c.E\flat qFqD$ (2); $c.E\flat sqDsqCcD$ (3) / 23.B.2: C (2) / 26 &c: *mercy on us* (some sources) / 31.A1.2–3: $c.FqGcE\flat$ (2) / 31.B.1–2: *cc* (2) / 32.A1.3–4: $qCqB\flat qCqD$ (3,4) / 34.A1.1 (and 36.A1.1): $c.CqB\flat mA$ (3,4) / 34.T.1 (and 36.T.1): $cA\flat cG$ (3).

2 A2.k-s: o (2) / 8.B.1–2: *cc* (2) / 10 &c: *spi^{q}ri^{q}tu^{c}al^c* (2) / 13.T.1–14.T.5: *songs^{m}and^c spi^{c}ri^{q}tu^{q}al^c* (2) / 22.B.2–3: *cc* (3) / 24.A1.1–2: *cAqBqB* (1) / 27 &c: *name of the Lord* (some sources) / 34.T.2–3: DD (2).

4 2.T.2: extra $cG\sharp$ (3) / 2.B.3: $cC\sharp$ (2) / 3.T.1: *mand^{c}de^{c}ments* (2,3) / 4.T.1: F$\sharp$ (1) / 4.T.2–3: *cc* (2,3) / 4.B.2–3: *cc* (2) / 5.rh.3,4: $^{A\natural}_{F\sharp}$ (2) / 8.A2.3: G$\sharp$ (1) / 16.T.3: B (1) / 18.T.3: *c.q* (1) / 19.A2.4: F (1) / 19.T.1–2: *cc* (1) / 19.B.4: $qD\sharp qE$ (1) / 22.B.4: *-ther* until 23.3 (2) / 23.B.4: *and^{c}I^{c}will^{c}love^{m}him* (2) / 24.T.1, 2nd time: $^{G\sharp}_{E}$ (3) / 27.rh.3: $^{A\natural}_{D\sharp}$ (2) / 28.B.1: *love^{c}him^{c}love^m* (2) / 31.T.2, 1st time: G$\sharp$ (3) / 31.T.2–33.T.3: *mine^{c}own^{m}self^{c}un^{c}m^{c}to^c* (1st time: 33.1 omitted) (3) / 31.T.2–33.T.3: *mine^{c}own^m self^{c}un^{c}to^{m}cc* (1st time: underlay of *unto* unclear) (2) / 32.T.2: C$\sharp$ (1) / 32.B.2–33.B.3: *and^{c}will^{c}show^{q}my^{q}self^{c}to^{c}him^m* (1) / 38.B.1–2: *c.q* (1) / 39.2–end, A1 and B: *myself unto him* (1) / 39.B.2–end: *my^{c}own^{c}self^{c}un^{c}to^c* (2) / 40: no indication of repeat (1) / 40, 2nd time, A2, T, B: no pause on 3 (1) / 40, organ, 2nd time: no pause on 3(2).

5 4.A2.3: *cc* (1) / 7.B.1: $m^F_D c^{E\flat}_C$ (3) / 8.A2.4: *with^{c}mu^{c}sic^{c}of^{c}con^c* (2) / 9.T.3: o (1,4) / 11.B.4: *and^{q}the^q* (1) / 12.A2.2: *and^{c}the^{c}Ho^{q}ly^q* (1) / 12.T.2: B$\flat$ (1) / 15.T.3: $c.A\flat qA\flat$ (4) / 18.1h.3: $c^{A\flat}_C c^{A\flat}_{A\flat}$ (3) / 21.A2.1: *heavn^c·ly^q* (1) / 21.A2.3: C (1) / 24.T.3–4: *cheerful* (1) / 36.T.1: o (1,4) / 39.rh.1: ^G_D (3) / 43.T.4–44.T.3: *and ever was* (1) / 46.T.2: C (1,2,3) / 52.B.2: missing (1) / 54.T.5: G (2).

15 28.T.1–2: *cc* (1) / 38.B1.3: missing (1) / 71.A.1: *c*-rest missing (1) / 72.T.2: $\sharp$ (1) / 80.T.2: extra $sF\sharp$ (1) / 80.T.2: $\natural$ plus extra sF (1).

Processed and printed by
Halstan & Co. Ltd., Amersham, Bucks., England